Illustrated by Angie Jones

Waiting
for
Baby

A Sibling
Visits the NICU

Balboa Press books may be ordered through booksellers or by contacting:

Balboa Press
A Division of Hay House
1663 Liberty Drive
Bloomington, IN 47403
www.balboapress.com
1-(877) 407-4847

Because of the dynamic nature of the Internet, any web addresses or links contained in this book may have changed since publication and may no longer be valid. The views expressed in this work are solely those of the author and do not necessarily reflect the views of the publisher, and the publisher hereby disclaims any responsibility for them.

ISBN: 978-1-4525-4549-3 (sc)

Library of Congress Control Number: 2012901443

Any people depicted in stock imagery provided by Thinkstock are models, and such images are being used for illustrative purposes only. Certain stock imagery © Thinkstock.

Printed in the United States of America

Balboa Press rev. date: 4/24/2012

BALBOA
PRESS
A DIVISION OF HAY HOUSE

Dedication

Matt and Nick, my amazing children, every day with you is a gift.

Mom & Dad and Matt, thank you for your
unconditional love and support.

Ethan and Ryan, you are the reason I had the
courage to move forward with this book.

-J.B.

For Kenzie, Kaitie, Seth, Emily and Kyle who inspire me every day. -A.J.

We're so excited for the new baby to come,

there will be snuggling, kissing, laughing and fun.

You can color him pictures with
blue, green and **red,**

read him books and touch his head.

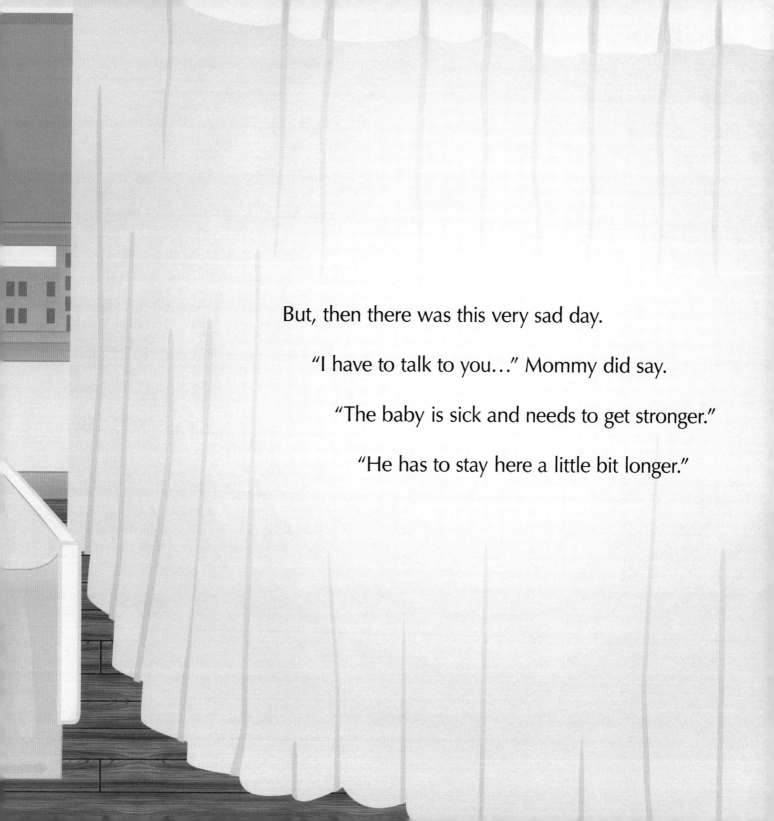

But, then there was this very sad day.

"I have to talk to you…" Mommy did say.

"The baby is sick and needs to get stronger."

"He has to stay here a little bit longer."

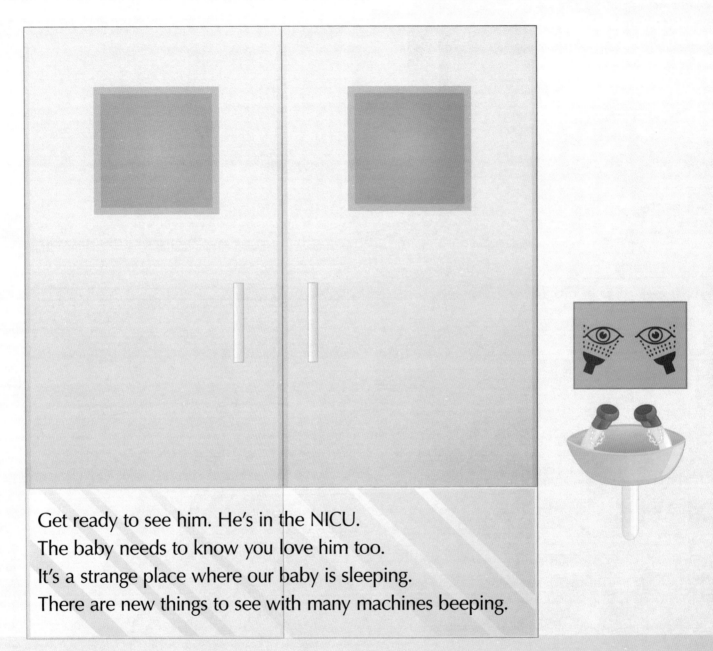

Get ready to see him. He's in the NICU.
The baby needs to know you love him too.
It's a strange place where our baby is sleeping.
There are new things to see with many machines beeping.

Wash your hands! Get them clean!
You must wear a gown before the baby is seen.
There are doctors and nurses watching the baby.
"Will I get to touch him?" you ask. I hope so, maybe...

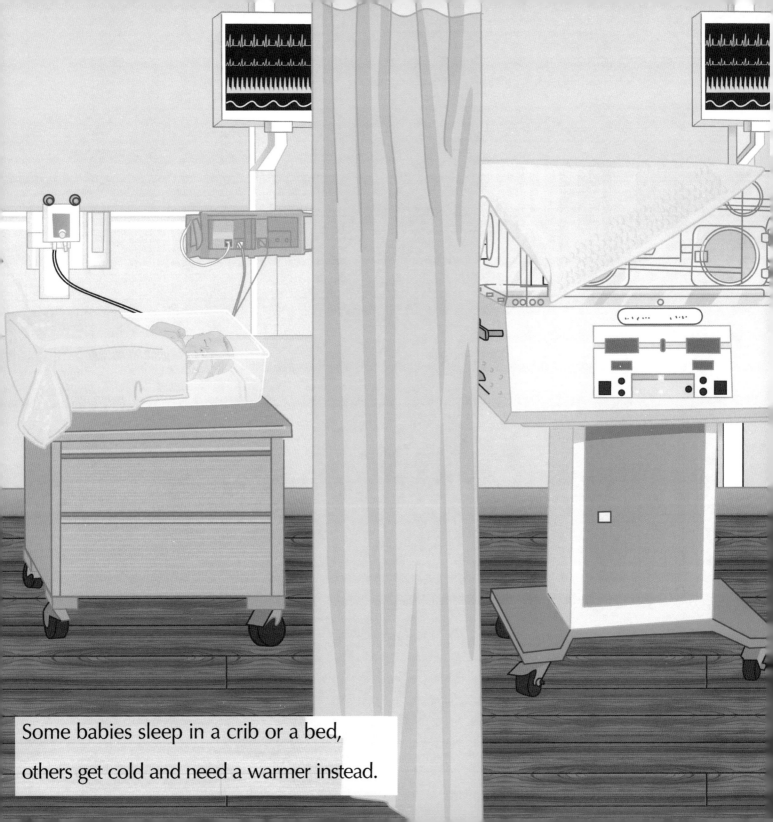

Some babies sleep in a crib or a bed,
others get cold and need a warmer instead.

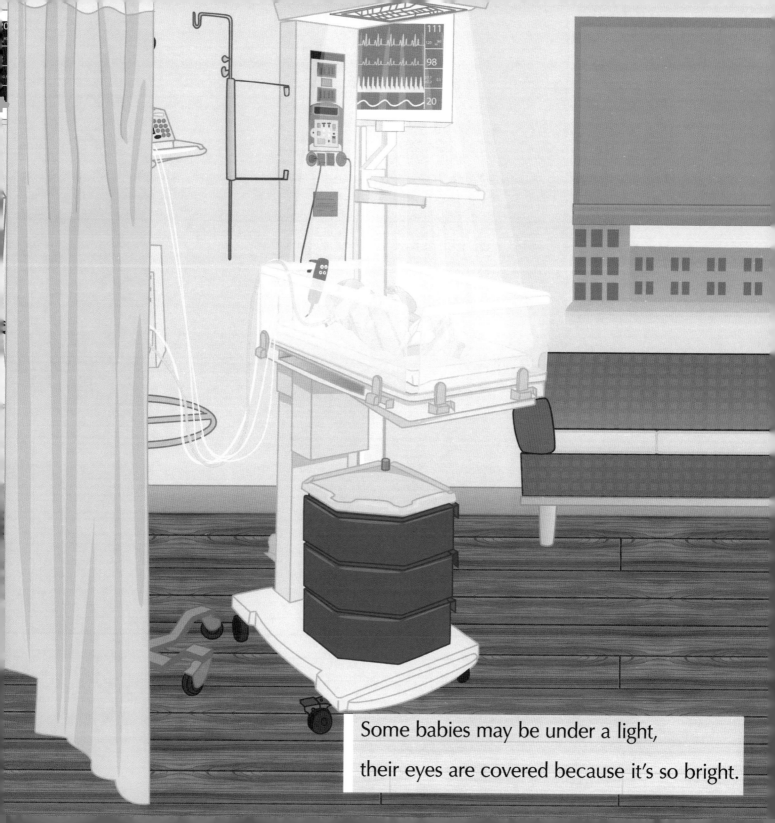

Some babies may be under a light,

their eyes are covered because it's so bright.

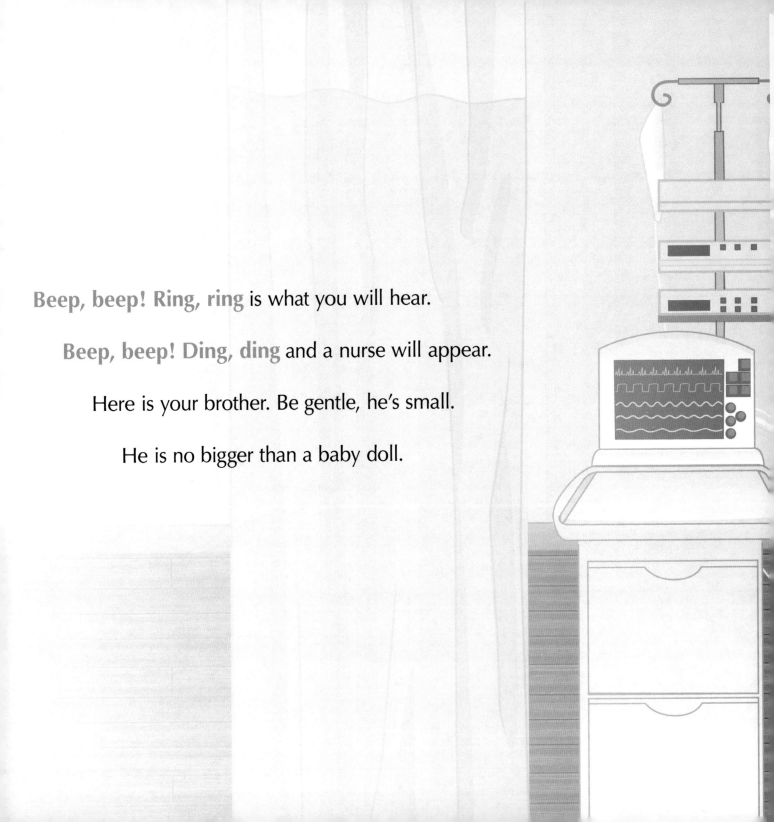

Beep, beep! Ring, ring is what you will hear.

Beep, beep! Ding, ding and a nurse will appear.

Here is your brother. Be gentle, he's small.

He is no bigger than a baby doll.

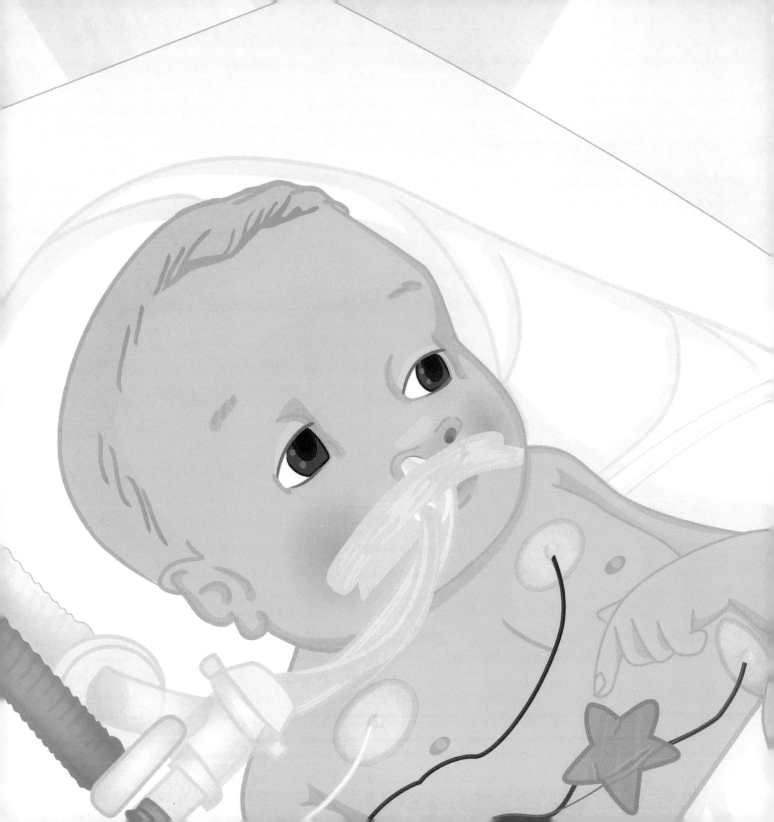

"What is that?" There may be tubes in his nose
or tubes in his mouth the size of a hose.
They are there to help the sweet babies breathe,
even though that might be hard to believe.

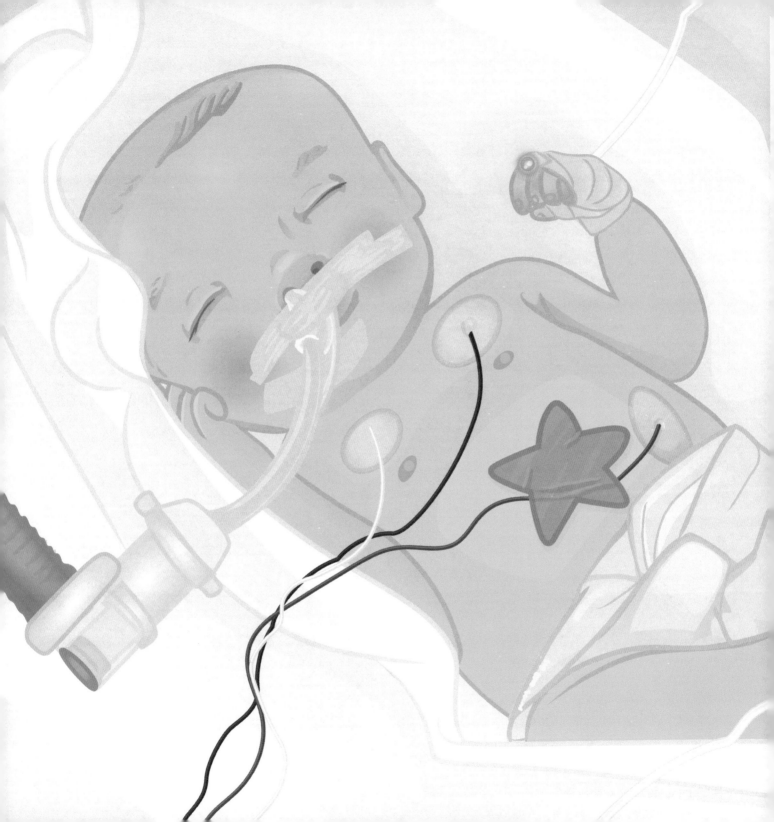

"Stickers on his chest?" "What are they for?"
"A red light on his foot?" "How can there be more?"
It may seem strange but those things check his heart.
They make the beep beep you heard from the start.

He may not use a bottle to eat.
So there may be IVs in his hands or his feet.
He needs more care for he needs to get strong.
Then you will see he'll be home before long.

"But why can't he come home?"

"He's lying there alone."

He needs a little rest and healing.

The question is… **"How are you feeling?"**

You may feel glad!

You may feel mad!

You may feel blue!

You don't know what to do!

Well, color him pictures with blue, green and **red.**

Read him books and touch his head.

He knows your voice. He knows your name.

He needs your love just the same.

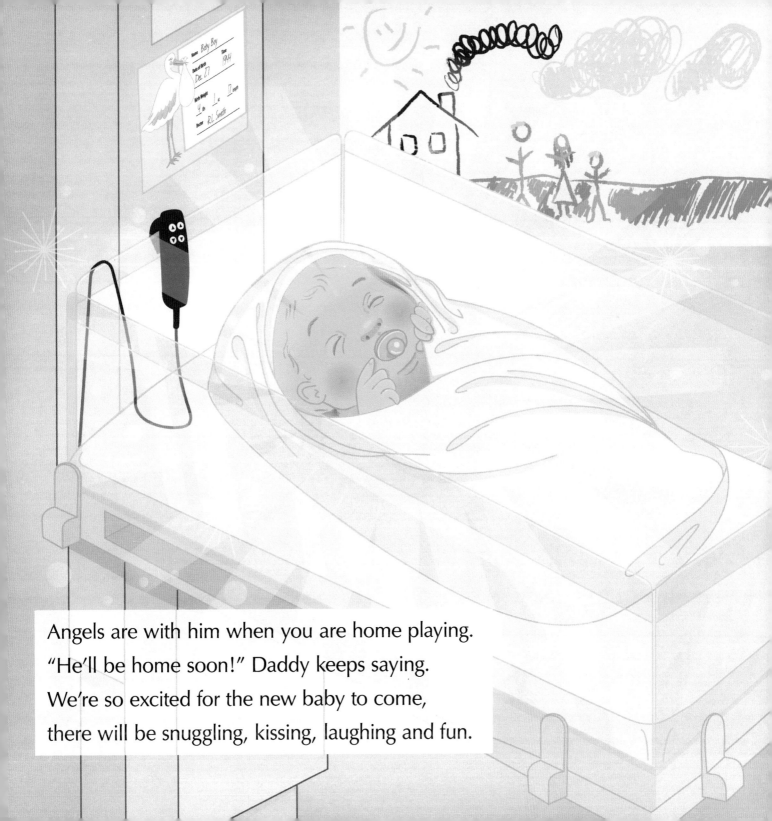

Angels are with him when you are home playing.
"He'll be home soon!" Daddy keeps saying.
We're so excited for the new baby to come,
there will be snuggling, kissing, laughing and fun.

Suggestions for empowering your child who is coping with having a new sibling in the Neonatal Intensive Care Unit...

- Have your child draw pictures for the baby and tape them to the baby's bed.

- Bring a small present to the baby.

- Have the baby "leave a present" for the sibling when he or she comes for a visit.

- Pick out family photographs to bring to the baby and tape them to the bed.

- Let your child pick out a few books to quietly read to the baby during a visit.

- Record the child's voice reading or telling a story to the baby.

- Ask the baby's nurse for a copy of the baby's footprints.

- Take a diaper home from the hospital so the child can practice changing a diaper.

- Make a scrapbook of pictures for the sibling to take to school or show other family members to help the child discuss what he saw, felt and learned.

- Look at photographs with your child when they were a newborn baby.

- Try to keep a normal routine for your older child to help them feel that their environment is safe and protected.

- Bring home blankets the baby was wrapped in so family pets can get used to the new baby's smell. Have your child talk to the family pets about the new baby.

Place a photograph of the new baby.

Draw a picture for the baby.

Made in the USA
San Bernardino, CA
21 April 2014